Contents

Acknowledgements

The author would like to thank her father, Peter, for encouraging her to follow in his own footsteps.

WordPerfect is a registered trademark of the WordPerfect Corporation, Orem, Utah.

Joanna Gosling is part of Writers Unlimited, Stamford.

How to use this Handbook

WordPerfect is one of the latest wordprocessing programs to be made available for the Personal Computers (PCs) that are finding their way into the smallest of offices. No longer is there a need for an expensive dedicated wordprocessing machine. Now there are a number of programs that provide all the features of the dedicated wordprocessor (and many more besides) and while the PC is not being used for wordprocessing it can be used for many other tasks necessary in a busy modern office. Many of the versatile programs to perform these tasks are featured in the Pitman Computer Handbook series.

This Handbook will give you a simple to use guide on the features of WordPerfect version 4.2 and once you have found your way around this Handbook then you will be able to make better use of the comprehensive manual supplied with the program. Many new computer users find that computer manuals present a formidable obstacle. They are fine if you know what you are looking for and how the manual is intended to be used. In other words the majority of manuals are produced for people who are rather more familiar with 'computer talk' than the average. Our Handbook is designed to provide a stepping stone between the user and the manual.

All the WordPerfect commands are listed and their use explained in a logical manner together with examples of documents produced by WordPerfect.

What WordPerfect Aims to Do

The program is started with the
WordPerfect system disk in drive A, if
you are using a twin floppy disk PC, and
typing WP. If you type WP/R instead you
will make the program run much faster.
This is only if you have in excess of
384K bytes of RAM. What happens is that
the program files are loaded into RAM
(Random Access Memory). By reading the
program files from RAM instead of from
disk the speed with which WordPerfect
runs is increased. There are other ways,
given in great detail in the manual, that
you can modify the way that WordPerfect
works. For example, unless you tell it
otherwise, WordPerfect will not
automatically make a backup copy of the
previous version of your document. To do
this you could type WP/R/S.

This command will automatically load
the program files into RAM and also
provide you with a SETUP menu where you
are asked in option 4 to define the
backup options. You can have a 'timed'
backup which is performed at regular time
intervals. This allows for the
possibility of power failures which could
lose all your text and puts the saved
text into a file called {WP}BACK.1 for
document 1 and {WP}BACK.2 for document 2.
Also in this option is the choice of
having your document backed up when you
save it. The backup file having a .BK!
extension.

After restarting WordPerfect you may
receive the message: Old Timed Backup
file exists: 1 rename; 2 delete.

Rename the earlier {WP}BACK file if you want to keep it.

You are first of all presented with a blank screen with the cursor, a flashing underline symbol, at the top left hand corner of the screen. At the bottom right of the screen are the symbols

Doc 1 Pg 1 Ln 1   Pos 10

telling you that you are on Line 1 of Page 1 of Document 1, because you can work on more than one document at once and can 'switch' screens. The cursor is at Position 10, which is 10 characters in from a hidden left hand margin that is provided for you automatically by WordPerfect.

All you need to do now is to type your document and it will appear on the screen as you type with the words automatically wrapping round from one line to the next when you come to the end of a line. WordPerfect defaults to provide you with a line 75 characters long with tabs at intervals of five characters. These can be changed by you as you for your document or permanently through the **SETUP** menu as you will see later. You should notice that the word at the right is **Pos**. If you press the 'Caps Lock' key you will see that this changes to **POS**. This is the way of telling that everything you type will be in capital letters until you press 'Caps Lock' again. You will notice that the cursor column number will become emboldened or underlined also according to the current situation.

4

Once you have typed in some text you
will want to have some practice in moving
about your document, possibly in order to
do some editing or insert some additional
words between parts of it. All work
starts from this screen, called the
template. You need not "zap" or name and
save your work until you are happy with
it. All WordPerfect functions are carried
out by means of the keyboard function
keys. They are used either alone or in
combination with the Alt, Shift or
Control key. There appears to be no real
pattern as to the functions controlled by
these keys. If you need help at any time
press F3. The template provided by
WordPerfect is an excellent 'aide-
memoire'. The cursor movement is
controlled by the keys on the keypad on
the right hand side of your keyboard. If
by any chance you find that when you
press one of these keys a number appears
instead of the cursor moving, press the
'Num Lock' key. This will put the keypad
into cursor mode. A list of the cursor
controls follows.

CURSOR CONTROL

To Tab Right	Tab
To Tab Left	Shift Tab
Go To	Ctrl Home
Word Left	Ctrl <---
Word Right	Ctrl -->
Screen Left	Home <---
Screen Right	Home -->
Screen Down	+/Home ↓
Screen Up	-/Home ↑
Page Down	PgDn
Page Up	PgUp
Start of text	Home,Home, ↑
End of text	Home,Home, ↓
Start of line (Text)	Home,Home, <---
Start of line (Codes)	Home,Home,Home, <---
End of line	Home,Home, -->
Hardspace	Home,Spacebar

WordPerfect provides not only the standard wordprocessing functions but also a sophisticated set of advanced features which include: spelling checker, thesaurus providing synonyms and antonyms, sorting, maths and merge features.

Insert
WordPerfect defaults to insert text automatically to the left of the cursor position. If you want to overtype text press the **Ins** key. This is a toggle. When typeover mode is in operation the word **Typeover** is displayed in the lower left hand corner of the screen.

6

Delete

Here is a list of the delete commands:

Del char at cursor - Del
Del char to left of cursor - Bkspce
Delete word - Ctrl Bkspce
Delete to end of line - Ctrl End
Delete to end of page - Ctrl PgDn
Delete marked block - Del Y

Escape

Although the Escape key may be used to cancel a command or remove a menu it is advised that you use the **Cancel** key (F1) instead.

Escape is used to repeat some WordPerfect features or a character n times. When you press **Esc** the n = 8 message is displayed. Overtype the 8 with the required number if required and select the feature or character you want to repeat, this will then be repeated n times. Here is a list of features that may be used with Escape:

Arrow keys
Delete Word
Macro
Page Up/Down
Screen Up/Down
Word Left/Right

Pages

WordPerfect defaults to give you a page break after 54 lines and a single row of hyphens is displayed across the screen at this point. To create a page break press **Ctrl Enter**, this produces a double row of hyphens across the screen. If you want to delete the break either position the

cursor at the start of the line above the
break and press **Del** or position the
cursor at the start of the line below it
and press **Backspace**.

Codes

When the format (i.e tabs, margins, page
length) is altered in the document the
commands are stored as codes which are
only viewed on your screen when
requested. For example, if you turn off
justification a [RT Just Off] code will
be embedded in the text. When you want to
take a look at the codes in order to
delete them or check the parameters you
need to use the Reveal Codes function
unique to WordPerfect (Alt F3).

Error Messages

Most error messages are self-explanatory
and relate the feature you are currently
using. You will receive an error message
when the disk is full and cannot save the
current file or retrieve the file
requested. At this point you can take a
look at the file directory (F5) and
delete unwanted files or replace the
current document disk with a new one and
save/retrieve the file to there.

WORDPERFECT FUNCTIONS AND THEIR USE

```
┌──────┐
│  F1  │              CANCEL
└──────┘
```

Use this command to cancel a function.
You will find that F1 will stop a command
such as **list files** (F5) or **sort** (Ctrl F9)
and return you to the current document.
   Cancel may also be used to cancel a
hyphenation request and to turn the block
feature off.

Undelete
When you press **Cancel** and there you are
not currently using a command that could
logically be cancelled the **Undelete**
command is understood.
   Up to three deletions are saved by
WordPerfect. A deletion is a group of
characters that were deleted at one time
before the cursor was moved. To retrieve
previously deleted text take the cursor
to the place where you want it to be
restored and press **F1**. The text you last
deleted is then shown at the cursor
position and you can restore this text or
look at a previous deletion and restore
that.

```
┌──────┐     ┌──────┐
│ Ctrl │     │  F1  │     SHELL
└──────┘     └──────┘
```

Use this command to leave your current
document and go out to the **shell** (DOS).
From here you are able to perform all the
usual DOS commands without having to

download to the A> and reload
WordPerfect. You should have COMMAND.COM
on the system disk for this function to
be operational. After you have completed
your work in DOS type **EXIT** to return to
the document.

| Shift | | F1 | SUPER/SUBSCRIPT |

Use this command to send text up or down
one third of a line (subscript/
superscript). Press Shift F1 1 to
superscript the following character or a
marked block. Press Shift F1 2 to
subscript the following character or a
marked block.

Overstrike
Press Shift F1 3 (overstrike) between two
characters to print the second of the
pair above the first. You could use this
command for accents.

Advance Text Up/Down
Shift F1 4 will shift subsequent text up
half a line. Use its opposite command,
Shift F4 5, to bring text down onto the
line once more. If you want to send
specific text down half a line then use
these same commands but in reverse order.
        Finally you can use the Shift F4 6
command to advance the printer a certain
number of lines on the page. This is
especially useful if you want to avoid
filling your document with blank lines.
Simply answer the prompt with the line
number to which you want the printer to

move before starting to print subsequent
text.

```
┌─────────┐      ┌─────────┐
│  Alt    │      │  F1     │      THESAURUS
└─────────┘      └─────────┘
```

Use this command to invoke the
WordPerfect Thesaurus. If you have a PC
with twin floppy disk drives the program
is kept on the Thesaurus disk. Replace
your document disk with the Thesaurus
disk before you start. Position the
cursor at any point in the word you want
to look up and press Alt F1. You may need
to type B:TH.WP before the Thesaurus can
be located by WordPerfect. You will be
offered synonyms, antonyms and verbs. A
maximum of three words and their
references can be displayed on a single
screen, side by side. See Figure 1.1 for
the result if you looked up the word
press.

Use the **Replace Word** option to replace
the word and then indicate by typing an
"N" for example, if you want **press** to
become **steam**. This removes the Thesaurus
from your screen so you can replace your
document disk and continue work.
   Use the **View Doc** option to remove
the highlight from the specified word in
your text, this does not take you out of
the Thesaurus.
   Use the **Look Up Word** option in order
to receive further information about one
of the words offered to you if it is
marked by a *. Simply type the
corresponding letter and a further column
or columns will be displayed. This time

11

Figure 1.1

press-(v)
1 A *cram
  B *crush
  C *force
  D *push
  E *shove
  5   *cluster
              *converge
              *crowd
2 F *compact
  G *compress
  H *concentrate
  I *constrict
  J *squeeze
press-(n)
6   fourth estate
            journalism
            media
            newspapers
3 K *flatten
  L iron
  M *smooth
  N *steam
  7   correspondents
              newsmen
              *reporters
4 O *induce

press-   press-(ant)
                      8 *pull
                         *expand
                         *wrinkle
                         *deter

            *persuade
            *provoke
            *urge

1 Replace Word; 2 View Doc; 3 Look Up Word; 4 Clear Column: 0

12

the Thesaurus marks these words with a *
and expects you to make your choice from
here.

Use the **Clear Column** option to
remove the extra column from the screen
containing information about a specified
word specified by the **Look Up Word**
option.

As soon as you are finished with the
Thesaurus press **CANCEL** or use the **Replace
Word** option to return to your document
and reinsert your document disk.

```
┌─────────┐
│  F2     │    SEARCH   FORWARDS
└─────────┘
```

Use this command when you want to do a
forward search for a character or string
in your current document. After you have
pressed F2 you will receive the following
prompt on your screen:

---> Srch:

     Enter the text you want to find
using spaces or hard carriage returns
where appropriate then press ESC to start
the search. The next time that you press
F2 your last entry will be the default.
If you want to take the cursor back to
its original position before the search
press the GO TO keys twice, i.e **Ctrl Home
Ctrl Home**.

```
┌─────────┐        ┌─────────┐
│Ctrl     │        │  F2     │    SPELL
└─────────┘        └─────────┘
```

The WordPerfect Speller has a dictionary
of at least 100,000 words and allows you
to check a block or page of text or a
whole document. Words are corrected
automatically and there is a facility for
you to look up alternatives both
phonetically and by pattern. You can add
or delete words from the dictionary and
do a word count too. The dictionary file
is called LEX.WP and is made up of a **main**
word list and a **common** word list, the
latter being used first. The dictionary
will also look in the {WP}LEX.SUP list

14

which is created as you add words to the
dictionary. The speller utility,
SPELL.EXE, helps you to maintain the
dictionary and even create your own more
specific dictionaries. If you are using a
hard disk make sure that LEX.WP and
SPELL.EXE are kept in the same directory,
if this is different from the directory
WP.EXE is in please specify this in the
SETUP menu. If you have a twin floppy
disk drive machine you need to have the
document onscreen, normally you would
retrieve it using the **Shift F10** command,
before replacing the data disk with the
Speller Disk and starting the speller,
this will be retained in memory while the
checking takes place and both WordPerfect
and Speller disks remain in the drives.

Start the speller with the **Ctrl F2**
command. When you are spell checking a
document the menu shown in Figure 2.1 is
displayed on your screen. Type 1 if you
just want to check the current word, 2 if
you want to check the page or 3 to check
the whole document. To check the document
word by word keep pressing 1. Number **4**
lets you change the name of the main and
supplementary dictionaries you want to
use. If you want to set up your own
personal dictionary you will need to use
the **Speller Utility**. This allows you to
alter the existing dictionaries or create
new ones and explained later on in this
section. Number **5** gives you the **Word or
Word Pattern:** message at the base of the
screen.

Figure 2.1

Check: 1 Word; 2 Page; 3 Document; 4 Change Dictionary; 5 Look Up; 6 Count

Figure 2.2

———————————————

A. es	B. ese	C. esp
D. esq	E. est	F. etc
G. sec	H. asc	I. ask

Not Found! Select Word or Menu Option (0=Continue)0
1 Skip once; 2 Skip; 3 Add Word; 4 Edit; 5 Look Up; 6 Phonetic

and gives you alternative spellings for the string you enter at this point. Use this to check your own spelling as you type. Alternatives are lettered, as in the Thesaurus, so press the corresponding letter to enter the word in your text. Finally option 6 counts all the words in the current document in a few seconds.

As soon as you have chosen one of the above options the spell check commences. The Not Found menu is displayed together with suggested alternatives, if any, once the first unrecognised word is located. If you were to look up the word ESC Figure 2.2 shows what you would see.

Press the corresponding letter of the alphabet to swap one of the alternatives for the original word. Press 1 to skip to the next word, press 2 to ignore any future occurrences of this word for this document; 3 will add the suspect word, in this case ESC, to the jug or personal dictionary you selected earlier. Press 4 to enter the correct spelling onto your screen if it does not appear in the list and follow this with Enter. 5 lets you look up spellings for an alternative word and 6 gives you phonetic alternatives.

If the spell check finds a double word the menu options allow you to delete one.

As soon as the spell check is finished you will receive a word count on the document or page checked. Replace the Spelling Check disk with the data disk if you use a twin floppy disk drive machine before continuing with your work.

Using the Speller Utility to Alter,
Change and Create Dictionaries
Place the dictionary data diskette in B
drive if you have a twin floppy machine
and type **spell b:** at the A>. If you have
a hard disk just type **spell** at the DOS
prompt. The menu shown in Figure 2.3 will
be displayed:

Figure 2.3

WordPerfect Speller Utility

0 - Exit
1 - Change/Create Dictionary
2 - Add words to dictionary
3 - Delete words from dictionary
4 - Optimize dictionary
5 - Display common word list
6 - Check location of a word
7 - Look up
8 - Phonetic look up

Selection:_

You may often need to select option 1 before performing any of the other options.

You can enter words into the specified dictionary straight from the keyboard if you select the second option. Make sure that you enter all the words for ALL the files before selecting Exit from this option as the adding process will always take about 20 minutes. If a word is added to the common word list it will automatically be added to the main word list.

Option 3 lets you delete words from the dictionary either from existing files or direct from the keyboard. Again, as in option 2 make sure that you have deleted ALL words before selecting Exit. The same rules apply in option 2 and 3.

The Optimize Dictionary option, number 4, is used after you have created a new dictionary so that you can see the

subsequent screenfuls of words. The
cancel key, F1, returns you to the menu.

Option 5 lets you view the common
word list and option 6 shows you whether
a specified word will be found in the
common or main list. The seventh and
eighth options work the same as the Look
Up and Phonetic Look Up in the Not Found
menu during a spell check.

Word Count
You can use the Speller program to count
the number of words in a file without
having to spell check the document too.
To do this you need to invoke the spell
check in the usual way and select the
Word Count option from the menu
displayed.

| Shift | | F2 | SEARCH BACKWARDS |

Use this command when you want to do a
backward search for a character or string
in your current document. After you have
pressed F2 you will receive the following
prompt on your screen:

<- Srch:

Enter the text you want to find
using spaces or hard carriage returns
where appropriate then press ESC to start
the search. The next time that you press
F2 your last entry will be the default.
If you want to take the cursor back to
its original position before the search
press the GO TO keys twice, i.e Ctrl Home
Ctrl Home.

| Alt | | F2 | REPLACE

Use this command when you want to replace
a specified character or string with
another specified character or string.
Replacement can be selective or
automatic. After the replace function is
invoked with the **Alt F2** command you are
asked whether you want to confirm each
replacement or have WordPerfect do it
automatically with the **w/confirm (Y/N)?**
prompt. You then receive the same prompt
as for forwards search --> **Srch:**. Type
the character or string you wish to find.
Press **Esc** or **F2** to display the **Replace
With?** prompt for replacement text. **Esc** or
F2 invokes the search and replace.
Remember to put a **space** on either side of
the string you wish to replace if you
want to make sure that only whole words
will be found and replaced.

Lowercase characters will match both
lowercase and uppercase characters but
uppercase characters will match uppercase
alone. Ctrl-X (^X) will match any
character except a function code, but
should not be the first character in a
string.

Block Replace
If you mark a block of text you can use
the search and replace function for the
specified text alone.

Features you can use in the replace string:

Advance Up/Down
Centre Page
Columns/On/Off
Hard Space
Hyphen
Hyphenation Cancel
Justification On/Off
Math On/Off
Math Operators
Merge Codes
Merge E/R
Overstrike
Soft Hyphen
Subscript
Widow/Orphan

```
F3
```
HELP

Use this command to access WordPerfect's
help screens. If you are using a machine
with twin floppy disk drives you will
probably find that the help file,
WPHELP.FIL, is kept on the Learning Disk
and will be asked to replace you data
disk with this one in order to continue.
Press any letter key and you will receive
a full list of commands and keys; press a
function key and you will receive help
about that function key. The **Enter** key or
space bar will return you to your
document.

```
Ctrl            F3
```
SCREEN

Use this command to access some of the
sophisticated features of WordPerfect.
You will be able to draw lines and boxes,
preprogram up to 250 further characters
by using the Alt or Ctrl keys in
conjunction with the letterkey of your
choice, use the window feature which
allows you to look at more than one
document on your screen at one time,
program the colours for your monitor or
switch between WordPerfect's automatic
reform feature or not. The screen menu is
shown in Figure 3.1.

Rewrite/auto Rewrite
Follow the **Ctrl F3** combination with **0** and
you are able to rewrite (or reform) the

Figure 3.1

0=Rewrite; 1=Window; 2=Line Draw, 3=Ctrl/Alt Keys; 4=Colors; 5=Auto Rewrite;0

Figure 3.2

1 = ‖ ; 2 = ‖‖; 3 = *; 4 = change; 5 = erase; 6 = move:

current screen of text that would not
normally be rewritten automatically.

The Auto Rewrite feature, option 5,
is a toggle command used to reform text
to use new margins, tabs or pitch. It
acts as soon as you press the down arrow.
Normally WordPerfect defaults to
automatically rewrite your text. If you
choose to turn this toggle command off
then the feature will not operate until
the time when you switch off the machine.
If you are working with columns it is
often easier not to rewrite your work
automatically. It is at such times that
you may wish to rewrite a paragraph of
text alone and so you would use the
Rewrite command each time that this is
needed.

Window
Option 1 is used so that you can open a
window on your current screen for the
secondary document. After you press the
Ctrl F3 1 keys you are asked:

Lines in this window: 24

The first document will use the
number of lines you specify at this point
and the window will use the lower portion
of the screen and have its own ruler line
to separate it from the first document.
Tabs are shown as black triangles and
margins with curly brackets. The Switch
command (Shift F3) then allows the cursor
to hop from window to window so that both
documents can be edited at the same time
and in view. If you want to close a
window you have to switch the cursor into
the window that contains the document you

want to keep onscreen, press the **screen
window** keys (Ctrl F3 1) and specify 24
lines for the window. If the first
document has 24 lines there is no room
for the second document and the window
has to close. Text in the secondary
document is not lost and may be viewed,
edited and saved in the normal way using
the **switch** command.

Line Draw
Line draw is accessed if you use option
2. You then receive the menu shown in
Figure 3.2.
          Press 1 and you can draw boxes or
single lines on the screen by moving the
cursor. Press 2 and lines are double. 3
lets you draw asterisks on the screen
while option 5 erases any lines that are
on the screen but option 6 allows you to
move the cursor about without disturbing
existing lines. Remember to turn the
automatic insert off and use **Typeover**
mode when filling in boxes.

Ctrl/Alt Keys
You are able to program the letterkeys so
that they produce additional characters
when used in conjunction with Ctrl or
Alt. If you press **Ctrl F3 3** you will see
the full list of symbols and characters
available. Each character is accessed by
means of a number, specified on the Y
axis, added to the number on the X axis.
So, if you want to be able to do the
letter e you would find the corresponding
number on the chart, in this case 130 and
then decide which letter combination
would be most suitable to invoke it, I
chose **Alt E**. So, when the chart is

onscreen press **Alt E**, this takes the
cursor into the box beside Alt E in the
upper chart, type the number 130 and
press **Exit** until you return to your
document. From now on you can press **Alt E**
to produce e in your text. Of course,
some of the characters you want to
produce will not work if your printer is
not physically able to produce them or if
it has not been programmed correctly.

Colours

If you are using a colour monitor you are
able to play about with the colours if
you use the **Ctrl F3 4** option. If you have
a graphics monitor you can decide how to
display bold and underline even if your
monitor does not use colour.

Shift		F3		SWITCH

Use this command to switch from the
primary to the secondary document screen
and back again. WordPerfect lets you work
on two documents simultaneously without
saving either of them. You can then
switch between the two simply and
quickly. Each document retains its
autonomy and either can be saved before
the other. You will not be able to leave
WP until both are actively saved or
"zapped". The window facility allows the
secondary and primary document, known as
doc 1 and **doc 2** to appear on the same
screen at the same time, one above the
other.

    If you use this command when you
have a marked block onscreen you are able

to change the case of the text in the
block to upper or lower case at the same
time.

Case Conversion
Once a block of text has been marked the
Shift F3 command invokes the **Case
Conversion** function rather than Switch.
Use this command to switch uppercase
letters to lowercase and vice versa.

| Alt | | F3 | REVEAL CODES

Use this command to receive a breakdown
of the codes that are embedded in your
current screen. Each hard carriage return
is displayed as [Hrt], each soft return
as [Srt]. Every time that tabs, margins,
pitch etc is altered this is recorded as
an embedded command only revealed when
the Alt F3 command is used. This facility
is useful because it will show you
exactly which keys you did press when you
are sure that you didn't! The codes are
displayed in a window in the lower half
of the screen. Remove the display of
codes from the screen by pressing Alt F3
once more.

Delete Codes
If you want to delete a code (and
therefore its function) reveal the codes
and delete this particular code from the
screen. Position the cursor in the space
in front of the code and press Del or in
the space after the code and press
Backspace.

Use this command to indent text to a
tabstop set on the ruler line. Press F4
once and text is indented to the first
tabstop. Press **F4** twice and text is
indented to the second tabstop. The
indent facility works for the following
tabstop regardless of the cursor
position. A hard carriage return or hard
page cancels the indent.
    If you want to delete an indent
retrospectively reveal the codes (Alt F3)
and delete them in the usual way.

Margin Release
Use the margin release keys (Shift Tab)
to take the cursor and text one tabstop
to the left. This produces text like the
illustration in Figure 4.1.

Figure 4.1

Each time that you press F4 text is
        indented one tabstop to the right.
        If you want to release the margin in
        the first line of the indented
        paragraph you will need to use the
        Shift and Tab keys. This does not
        affect the remainder of the indented
        paragraph.

```
┌─────────┐      ┌─────────┐
│  Ctrl   │      │   F4    │      MOVE
└─────────┘      └─────────┘
```

Use this command to move, copy or delete
text or columns. The menu shown in Figure
4.2 is displayed as soon as the **Ctrl F4**
key combination is pressed.

Move/Copy/Delete Sentence
To move a sentence for example place the
cursor in that sentence and press **Ctrl F4**
1. The sentence will become highlighted
and you receive a further choice:

1 Cut; 2 Copy; 3 Delete 0

Cut
This will remove the highlighted sentence
from the screen and store the sentence in
temporary memory until it is recalled
onscreen at the appropriate cursor
position with the **Retrieve Text** command
(**Ctrl F4 5**).

Copy
This will store the highlighted sentence
in temporary memory until you want to
retrieve it in the same way.

Delete
This will delete the sentence from your
screen. Options 2 and 3 for the moving of
paragraphs and pages work in the same
way.

Move/Copy/Delete Block of Text
When you want to move a piece of text
other than that specified you will need

to mark it as a block before invoking the move facility.

   This command is used when you want to cut and paste text.

Rectangle
Use the **rectangle** feature to mark a rectangle of text as a block and move, copy or delete it.

Copying and Moving Columns
If you want to move a column it must first be marked as a block. When you start to do this you will think that the column is not being marked, but instead, the whole block. Just start in the top left hand corner and end in the lower right. As soon as the **move** command is invoked (Ctrl F4) the column will be shown correctly as a narrow block and the menu shown in Figure 4.3 is displayed.

   Press 4 to Cut/copy the column and then retrieve it in the normal way with Ctrl F4 4, which will retrieve the column. The same menu is displayed when you move a block of any type.

Append
The **Append** feature will copy the block to the end of the disk file you specify at the **Append to:** prompt. If you want to save a block of text to a completely new file you need to use the **Save** function, see section on F10.

Figure 4.2

Move 1 Sentence; 2 Paragraph; 3 Page; Retrieve 4 Text; 5 Column; 6 Rectangle

Figure 4.3

1 Cut Block; 2 Copy Block; 3 Append; 4 Cut/copy Column; 5 Cut/Copy Rectangle: 0

| Shift | | F4 | INDENT TO LEFT AND RIGHT |

Use this command as for INDENT. This time
the hanging paragraph will move in to the
first and last tabstops on the ruler
line. Press **Shift F4** twice and text is
indented to the second and penultimate
tabstop, and so on. The indent facility
works for the following tabstop
regardless of the cursor position. A hard
carriage return or hard page cancels the
indent.

   If you want to delete an indent
retrospectively reveal the codes (Alt F3)
and then delete the code using **Backspace**
or **Del**.

| Alt | | F4 | BLOCK |

Use this command to specify portions of
text to work with. This feature is used
mostly for cut and paste operations,
copy, deletion and printing of text and
writing text out to different files in
addition to many other functions. To
specify a block start with the cursor at
the first character in the block and
press the block keys, Alt F4. The words
block on flash in the lower left hand
corner of the screen. As you move the
cursor down the text it passes becomes
highlighted, this is the block. You can
move the cursor quickly by specifying the
next character for the highlight to move
to. **Enter** for example will highlight the
paragraph, until the next hard return.

33

Similarly a period will take you to the
end of the sentence and so on. You can
highlight the page if you use the PgDn
key in its various combinations or **Home**
Home ↓ to go to the end of the document.
     When you have a marked block on
screen some of the menus will alter
accordingly. For example, if a block is
marked and you press the **Del** key you will
receive the prompt **Delete Block Y/N ?**.
Similarly if a block is marked and you
press the **Save** key you will receive the
prompt **Block Name:** so that the block may
be written out to a new file and so on.

Use this command to undertake all disk
management operations. You can change the
default directory, check for files that
contain a string or word, take a look at
a document file or another directory,
retrieve, delete, rename, print or copy a
file and also retrieve an ASCII file.
    When you first press **F5** the name of
the default drive or directory is
displayed on the screen, i.e. A:*.*.
Press **Enter** to receive this file
directory or type the name of the
directory you wish to work with and press
Enter. Type B: and press **Enter** to see
what files are on the disk in drive B or
C:\john to see the files in the directory
called "john" on the hard disk or even
B:*LET.* to see files on B with **LET** as
part of their name, and so on. Type = to
change the default directory or create a
new one to your following specification.
The List Files screen appears with a
header that tells you the date, time,
size of document memory, the current
directory and, perhaps most useful of
all, the amount of disk space that
remains. Files are listed in alphabetical
order. Use the block cursor to specify
the file you want to work with. The file
management options are as shown in Figure
5.1.

Figure 5.1

1 Retrieve; 2 Delete; 3 Rename; 4 Print; 5 Text In;
6 Look; 7 Change Dir; 8 Copy; 9 Word Search; 0 Exit: 6

Figure 5.2

Date: 1 Insert Text; 2 Format; 3 Insert Function: 0

Retrieve

Use this option to call the document
marked by the block cursor into your
blank template. Files can also be
retrieved via the **Shift F10** command.

Delete

Use this option to delete the marked
document or directory from disk. The
Delete "filename" (Y/N)? prompt appears
before deletion takes place. Type **Y** to
delete the file or **any other key** if you
change your mind.

Rename

Use this option to rename the marked file
by entering the new filename.

Print

Use this option to print the marked file.
The print parameters are already embedded
in the text of the file and so the
document is sent to the printer directly.

Text In

Use this option to bring a copy of the
ASCII (or DOS text) file onto the
template prepared for WordPerfect.

Look

Use this option to take a quick look at
the start of the marked file. It cannot
be edited in this form so you are asked
to **Press any key** to continue. The cursor
keys will let you scroll through the
document. If you have the block cursor on
a directory and use this option you are
able to look at the contents of that
directory.

Change Dir
Use this option to change the default
directory or create a new one. Amongst
the files listed you will see that
WordPerfect has two files called **PARENT**
and **CURRENT** used by DOS to link the
directories with the root.

Delete Dir
Directories are deleted through the List
Files screen. Highlight the directory
name, select the **Delete** option and
proceed. A directory cannot be deleted
until it is empty.

Copy
Use this option to copy the marked file
to another file, directory or drive. You
can enter a new filename to create a new
file or use existing names in new
directories or drives.

Word Search
Use this option to display all the files
in the current directory that contain one
or more words, or have words that match a
pattern. Enclose words in double
quotation marks. Wild cards, * and ? may
be used in addition to semicolons, spaces
and commas as logical operators (AND, OR
respectively). For example you could look
for files that contain **March,April** (March
OR April); **March;April** (March AND April);
Mar* (All words beginning with Mar);
??r?? (Words of 5 characters, the middle
being r) or **"Married Wom?an"** (Married
Woman/Women when together in the
document) and so on.

Exit
Use this option, **Cancel** or **Enter** to
return to your template/document.

```
 Ctrl        F5         TEXT IN/OUT
```

Use this command to save your current
document in ASCII format (DOS) or to call
a document in from ASCII to your screen.
This is useful when you want to convert
your document into another program at a
later stage or to prepare the document to
send to an output device. When a document
is saved into ASCII all WordPerfect
formatting codes are deleted. When you
want to call text in it is sensible to
set the margins wider than necessary
before it is retrieved in order to
preserve the current format. Print a DOS
text file using printer 6 so that it is
printed to **disk** preserving formatting
commands.
      This command is also used to create
or edit a document summary or comment,
both of which are useful for reference
purposes.
      The menu which appears at the Ctrl
F5 command is self-explanatory.

Locked Documents
Documents may be locked with a password.
A locked document must be printed from
the screen. The first time you lock a
document use the **Text In/Out** key
beforehand and select option 4 (Save
locked document). Enter your password
twice, as requested. It does not appear
on your screen so you type it twice to

prevent mistyping. A password can contain up to 75 characters. Now enter a name for the file and it will be saved.

To retrieve a password protected document use the **Shift F10** or **Retrieve** commands in the usual way but you will be asked to enter the password first.

To unlock a document use **Ctrl F5 5** and enter the filename and the password for the document.

Be careful! If you forget the password there is no way you can retrieve the file.

Shift		F5		DATE

Use this command to insert the current date and time into your document. If you did not set them during booting up they will be entered as 00:00. You are able to choose which format you want to use for the date, whether it be text or code. A code will automatically put the current date into the document when it is printed. After you press **Shift F5** the menu shown in Figure 5.2 is displayed.

Option 1 inserts the date as you entered it at "boot up" in words, i.e. January 20, 1987. If you want the format of the text to be different from this select option 2 and alter the format according to the list given, as shown in Figure 5.3.

Figure 5.3

Date Format

Character	Meaning
1	Day of the month
2	Month (number)
3	Month (word)
4	Year (all four digits)
5	Year (last two digits)
6	Day of the week (word)
7	Hour (24-hour clock)
8	Hour (12-hour clock)
9	Minute
0	am /pm
%	Include leading zero for numbers less than 10 (must directly precede number)

Examples: 3 1,4= December 25, 1984
          %2/%1/5 (6)= 01/01/85 (Tuesday)

Date Format: 3 1,4

Follow this chart to set the date in your chosen format.
Option 3 will insert a function code into your text that is able to update the date. The date (and time if requested) will then appear each time the document is retrieved and at print time.
Ostensibly this date looks the same as that created by option 1, however option 1 does not alter according to the day it is printed and option 3 does.
When you want to enter the date during a merge you will enter the date in a different way using Alt F9 D, see section on Alt F9.

41

```
╔═══════════╗      ╔═══════════╗
║   Alt     ║      ║    F5     ║       MARK TEXT
╚═══════════╝      ╚═══════════╝
```

Use this command to help you to create
outlines by automatically inserting
paragraph numbers, to insert paragraph
numbers, to mark text for redlining.
Redlining produces a vertical line down
the left hand side of text to signify
that the text is being considered for
inclusion or deletion. You are also able
to mark text for indexes, lists and
tables of contents and then generate
them. The **block** feature may also be used
in conjunction with marks. The Mark Text
menu is illustrated in Figure 5.4.

Outline
This feature automatically inserts
paragraph numbers to create an outline.
You can have up to seven levels in an
outline. If you edit or move paragraphs
subsequently they will be renumbered
automatically. An outline number appears
on screen because of a [Par#] code. To
delete the number delete the code. Figure
5.5 shows an example of an outline.

Figure 5.4

1 Outline; 2 Para #; 3 Redline; 4 Short Form; 5 Index; 6 Other Options

Figure 5.6

Mark for: 1 ToC; 2 List; 3 Redline; 4 Strikeout; 5 Index; 6 ToA: 0

Figure 5.5

I.This is section one, as you can see the
text wraps round and the paragraph is
numbered by pressing Enter.
     A.By pressing Enter and then Tab the
first subsection is numbered too.
     B.So, the number of tabs you press
determine the level of numbering.

II.This is section two but maybe it would
look nicer if the indent command were
used.
     A.   Press Tab followed by Indent
           and the result is much
           prettier.
           1.   And so on and so on and so
                 on and so on and so on...

Choosing the Numbering Style
Select the style of numbering you would
like to use from the Options option from
the Alt F5 menu. Choose the Define
Paragraph/Outline Numbering option from
this menu (see Figure 5.7) and select the
style you require. Outline style is I A 1
a (1) (a); Paragraph style is 1 a i (1)
(a) (i); Legal style is 1. 1.1   1.1.1
1.1.2   2.   2.1 and so on. You can also
invent your own style of numbering.

Starting Outlines
To start creating your outline switch the
outline toggle ON by pressing Alt F5 1.
Each time you press Enter a number will
appear. As you press Tab the subsection
number is displayed. To indent the
paragraph press Indent after the Tab key.

Stopping Outlines
To stop the outline feature press the Alt
F5 1 command once more and the outline
message will stop flashing at the base of
the screen.

Aligning Paragraph Numbers
To number paragraphs and align the
numbers to the tab in addition to the
text itself so that numbers line up as
follows:

  I.
 II.
III.

Use the Ctrl F6 command to align the
tabs. Then press Alt F5 2 Enter to insert
an automatic paragraph number that aligns
to the tab. Press space bar twice to
allow for the space before the text. Type
a period to stop the tab align feature,
Press backspace to delete it. Overstrike
the second space (Shift F1 3) and indent
the paragraph (F4).

Deleting Outlines/Paragraph Numbers
To delete the number you must delete the
corresponding code [Par#].

Paragraph Numbers
Use the paragraph numbering option from
the Alt F5 menu to number paragraphs
automatically. There are seven levels
available. Type the level you wish to use
after the Alt F5 2 command if different
from the default, starting at level one.
    If you redefine the numbering style
after you have been numbering previous

paragraphs the numbers will default to
start at level one once more.

Redline and Strikeout
The redline and strikeout features allow
you to indicate text that you may like to
delete. The redline feature marks the
line(s) of suggested text with a vertical
line at the left margin and the strikeout
feature puts an horizontal line through
each specified character. When text is
redlined a + appears beside the **Pos** in
the status line. This is a toggle
command. When text is struck out a -
appears beside the **Pos** in the status
line. This too is a toggle.
      If you want to redline or strikeout
existing text you need to mark the text
as a block first.

Index
WordPerfect will generate you an index
from the text in your document. Headings
and subheadings are available. Mark each
word you want in the index using the **Alt
F5 5** command. At this point you can
select whether the marked text is to be
entered for the heading or subheading or
the replacement text for this category.
      If you want to enter more than one
word to the index the whole string must
be marked as a block first. This invokes
a slightly different menu.
      When the cursor is at the point
where you want the index to appear,
define the numbering style using the **Alt
F5 6 1** command and generate the index
using the **Alt F5 6 8** command.
      Each time that an index is created

for a document all previous versions will be replaced with the new one.

Table of Contents/List/Table of Authorities

A table of contents places items in chronological order and with the level of the section. A list is just a simple list, also in chronological order, but without levels. An index, of course, places items in alphabetical order with headings and subheadings.

All these features display the page number of the marked text.

To include items in a table of contents or list each word or string is marked as a block first. The menu shown in Figure 5.6 appears when you press **Alt F5**. Select whether the marked text is for the ToC or List and continue until you have marked all the words in your document. Define the ToC/List and then generate it at the point where you want it to appear.

Tables of authorities will provide full form references to short forms in the text and group them at the place where the ToA is generated. This feature could be used if you want to make references in the text to a bibliography. Again text is marked first and then added to the ToA (Alt F5 6). The **full form** will appear in the bibliography, for example, and the **short form** appears in the text. Define the ToA before you generate it from the **Options** option in the **Alt F5** menu.

Figure 5.7

1 – Define Paragraph/Outline Numbering
2 – Define Table of Contents
3 – Define List
4 – Define Table of Authorities
5 – Define Index
6 – Remove all Redline Markers and all Strikeout Text
      from Document
7 – Edit Table of Contents
8 – Generate Tables and Index

48

Options

The options menu is shown in Figure 5.7.
Use this menu to define the parameters
for all outlines, redline, paragraph
numbering, tables of contents, index,
list and other numbering and display
styles.

| F6 | BOLD

Use this command to produce text that
prints in boldface and appears on the
screen in highlight. The bold command is
a toggle and reveals the code [B] at the
start of boldface and [b] at the end. In
order to delete bold you need to delete
the [B] code. If codes are not revealed
and you try to delete an embedded code by
using the backspace or **Del** key the
following prompt will appear onscreen:
Delete Bold (Y/N) ? N. Type **n** or any key
other than **Y** to leave the bold code.
　　If you want to embolden text
retrospectively you need to mark it as a
block first, see section on Alt F4.

| Ctrl | | F6 | TAB ALIGN

Use the tab align feature to line up text
or numbers to the right (flush right) or
use the next tab stop as a decimal tab.
Before you can use this feature you have
to have the relevant tab stop set on the
ruler line (see Shift F8). Press **Ctrl F6**
and the following message is displayed on
your screen:

Align Char = .

　　If you reveal the codes you will see
that the aligned characters are set
inside **[A] [a]** tags. This command saves
you having to set decimal tabs on the
ruler line in advance. The tab align

feature is also accessed if you press
Shift F8 6.

| Shift | | F6 | | CENTRE |

Use this command to centre subsequent
text between right and left margins one
line at a time. If your text becomes too
wide for the margins press ESC to
hyphenate the text when requested.

Text will only centre if there is a
hard return at the end of the line. If
text is not at the left hand margin
before the centre command is pressed text
will be centred at the cursor position.

To centre an existing line take the
cursor to the start of the text and press
Shift F6.

Centre Column
To centre a column heading place the
cursor in the centre of the column, press
Shift F6 and move the cursor downwards.
To centre a column retrospectively mark
it as a block first.

| Alt | | F6 | | FLUSH RIGHT |

Use this feature to align text flush
against the right hand margin. This
feature is useful for dates or perhaps
business headings. As soon as you press
Alt F6 the cursor hops to the right hand
margin and text is lined up to here. This
code takes precedence over other codes.

51

Text entered before a flush right code on that line may disappear.

You can adjust text so that it is flush right retrospectively if you mark the text as a block, press **Alt F6** and then **Y**.

Use this command to save your current
document and either exit WordPerfect and
return to DOS or get yourself a blank
template to work on.

If you use the **Shell** command you
will need to type **exit** to return to your
document. When you press **F7** you receive
the following prompt onscreen:

Save Document? (Y/N) Y

Press **Enter** to save it if you want
to keep this version. If the document has
been named and saved previously you will
be asked to confirm the name, for
example:

Document to be saved: B:LETTER1

Overtype this name if it is
incorrect and press **Enter** to continue. If
the document has been saved under this
name beforehand you will have to replace
it with this newer version and so type **Y**
as the response to the next prompt:

Replace? (Y/N) N

Once the file is saved you will
receive a final prompt:

Exit WP? (Y/N) N

Press **Y** to return to DOS. Any other
key will remove the saved document from

your screen and give you a blank
template.

If you change your mind at any time
Cancel will stop the **Save** command.

| Ctrl | F7 | FOOTNOTE |

Use this command for both footnotes and
endnotes. A footnote appears at the base
of the same page as its reference number,
endnotes appear together at the very end
of the file. Footnotes and endnotes will
be numbered automatically by WordPerfect.
You can have both sorts of note in the
same document.

To use this feature you need to
start with the cursor at the point where
you want the reference number to be
printed for the note, then press **Ctrl F7**.
The menu shown in Figure 7.1 is
displayed.

Select 1 or 5 to create your note
and you will receive a special screen
into which you type the text for the
note. The current number is displayed.
Press **F7** when you are finished and that
number is shown onscreen to remind you
there is a foot/endnote there. Delete the
number to delete the note text.

A note may be up to 16,000 lines
long - plenty for anyone! However, the
reveal codes command (Alt F3) will only
show you the first 50 lines of the note.

When your text contains a note
WordPerfect automatically adjusts the
number of lines that will fit on the page
so that there is room for the note.

54

If you ever want to edit an existing note select option 2 or 6 from the footnote menu. Confirm the number of the note to alter and the note text will be displayed in its special screen as before. Edit the text in the normal way and press F7 to end.

Endnotes will normally print at the very end of your document. If you want them to print on a separate page you need to end the document with a hard page break (Ctrl Enter).

If you want footnote numbering to start at a particular number position the cursor to the left of the appropriate number and select option 3 from the footnote menu. The following prompt will be displayed:

Ftn # ?

Type the new number and press Enter.

Footnote Options

The footnote options are accessed via option 4 from the footnote menu, see Figure 7.2.

For the first two options use the number 1 for single spacing, 1.5 for one and a half spacing and so on. The third option refers to the number of lines of footnote that have to stay on the same page as the reference number if the footnote has to be split. Option 4 allows you to start new footnote numbers on each page if you would like. Options 5, 6 and 7 are explained onscreen. The eighth option lets you decide whether you want blank lines to be inserted between the text and the notes if the notes do not

Figure 7.1

1 Create; 2 Edit; 3 New #; 4 Options; 5 Create Endnote; 6 Edit Endnote:0

Figure 7.2

1 – Spacing within notes
2 – Spacing between notes
3 – Lines to keep together
4 – Start footnote numbers each page
5 – Footnote numbering mode
6 – Endnote numbering mode
7 – Line separating text and footnotes
8 – Footnotes at bottom of page
9 – Characters for notes
A – String for footnotes in text
B – String for endnotes in text
C – String for footnotes in note
D – String for endnotes in note

Figure 7.3

1 Full Text; 2 Page; 3 Options; 4 Printer Control; 5 Type-thru; 6 Preview: 0

take up the assigned number of lines. The
default is not to do this. The ninth
option deals with the sort of characters
you want as the reference in the text,
you can have numbers or asterisks. Unless
specified at this point the numbers will
simply be doubled or triple after they
have been used once. The letter options
relate to the style you want to use for
the notes in the text and in the note
itself. Press the underline key (**F8**) at
this point and notes will be underlined.
You can also use superscript here.

If you change any margins in your
document they will also need to be
changed for each note. The easiest way to
do this is by doing a word count through
the spell check facility as this resets
margins for you. Alternatively you could
edit the relevant note(s) and exit
immediately. You could create a macro to
do this for you for each note.

| Shift | | F7 | PRINT |

Use this command to print the document
that is currently on your screen. You are
able to specify whether you print the
current screen page (**page**) or the full
text (**full text**). If you have marked a
block on the screen you can print this
block using the **Shift F7** command. You are
also able to print a file different from
the one onscreen (option 4) and specify
the relevant pages for that one too. The
print menu is shown in Figure 7.3.

Options

Use this option from the menu to choose
which will be the output printer, how
many copies you want and the binding
width (in tenths of an inch).

Printer Control

Use this option to set printing
parameters relating to topics such as
your printer and hopper feed. The screen
that is displayed is illustrated in
Figure 7.4.

Print Parameters 1, 2 and 3

The first screen that appears asks
you to select print options (1), display
available printers and fonts (2) and
select printers (3).

Option 1 has the same effect as
option 3 from the main printer menu.

Option 2 will give you a list of
about 30 or so printers that WordPerfect
can work with for you to select from.

Option 3 is the most complex and
shows the printers that are in the
A\WPRINTER.FIL. For each of these
specified printers there are further
parameters listed as soon as you press
Enter. First you get a list of available
ports. After you make your selection
Enter gives you the choice between using
continuous, hand fed or sheet fed paper.
If you are using a sheet feeder of some
description press Enter again and you
will receive more details relating to
this. The lines that come between pages
defines the amount of scrolling necessary
between sheets, 24 lines is normal. You
can select the column position for the
left margin too, and 10 is standard.

Figure 7.4

Printer Control

1 – Select Print Options
2 – Display Printers and Fonts
3 – Select Printers

C – Cancel Print Job(s)
D – Display all Print Jobs
G – "Go" (Resume Printing)
P – Print a Document
R – Rush Print Jobs
S – Stop Printing

Selection: <u>0</u>

Current Job

Job Number: n/a
Job Status: n/a
message: The Print Queue is empty

Page Number: n/a
Current Copy: n/a

Job List

<u>Job</u> <u>Document</u>   <u>Destination</u>   <u>Forms and Print Options</u>

Additional jobs not shown:0

Finally you can specify the number of
bins in your sheet feed. Press **Enter** to
return to the earlier menu once more.
These parameters will be fixed for each
document until you change them or the
printer.

Print Parameters C, D, G, P, R and S
The options at the right hand side of the
Printer Control menu control the print
queue and allow you to stop and start the
printing process.

Cancel Print Jobs
Press C at this menu, see Figure 7.3, to
stop printing. Check that the correct job
number is displayed and press **Enter** if it
does not stop straight away. You know
when the buffer is empty because the
Print Queue is Empty message is shown in
the message line. Once a print job has
been cancelled you may need to "Go" next
time that you send something to print.

Display all Print Jobs
Use this option to check the state of the
print queue. You may need to **Rush** an
important job to the front of the queue.

"Go" (Resume Printing)
Use this command to start printing a
document that you **stopped** or to print a
later document that does not print
immediately.

Print a Document
Use this option to print a document other
than the one on your screen. You can
specify which pages you want to print
from here too.

Rush Print Jobs
This command allows you to rush a print job to the front of the print queue.

Stop Printing
Use this option to stop printing a document temporarily. Use "Go" to resume printing.

Type-thru
Use this option to use WordPerfect like a typewriter. Choose whether to send text to the printer one at a time or by line. Text entered in type-thru mode is not saved. The sixth option, preview, shows you the document or page as it will be printed, with the agreed margins page by page.

Print from List Files Menu
Entire documents can be printed from the List Files menu. The **Print Format** parameters set for that document will still adhere but the current default **Print Options** will be used.

| Alt | F7 | MATH/COLUMNS |

Use this command to perform simple mathematical calculations on horizontal or vertical columns of tabbed figures and to set up newspaper or parallel styles columns for text. Figure 7.5 shows the **Math/Columns** menu.

Maths

There are up to 24 columns available (A-X) and you set the style for their contents from the math definition option in the math/column menu, see below:

Before you can start to enter text, figures and calculations you need to set the tabs for the columns, a column will only be understood as such if the text is preceded by a tab. So, press **Shift F8 1** and clear all the existing tabs before setting new ones, see section on Shift F8 for further information about setting tabs.

Before you can start to use the "mini spreadsheet" WordPerfect offers and after you have set the tabs you need to define the maths columns, so choose option **2**. The screen shown in Figure 7.6 is displayed.

The first line gives you the letter that defines each of the vertical columns. The following 3 lines need to be filled with information about the type of data that is to go into each of the columns you are going to need. This is explained at the base of the screen. A calculation (0) refers to the spot where you will enter the formula for that cell (such as A*B). As soon as you overtype the 2 with a 0 the letter referring to that column is displayed beside the Calculation section of the

Figure 7.5

1 Math On; 2 Math Def; 3 Column On/Off; 4 Column Def; 5 Column Display: 0

Figure 7.6

Math Definition   Use arrow keys to position cursor

Columns   ABCDEFGHIJKLMNOPQRSTUVWXYZ

Type   2222222222222222222222222222

Negative Numbers   ((((((((((((((((((((((((

# of digits to   2222222222222222222222222222
the right (0-4)

Calculation   1
Formulas   2
              3
              4

Type of Column:
  0 = Calculation   1 = Text   2 = Numeric   3 = Total

Negative Numbers:
  (= Parenthesis   (50.00)   - = Minus Sign   -50.00

Press EXIT when done

63

screen, type A*B and press F7. The
following symbols are used for maths:

*	Multiplication
/	Division
+	Addition
-	Subtraction
+	Use this alone to add all the figures in the row
+/	Use this alone to produce the average the numbers
=	Use this alone to add the numbers in the total columns
=/	Use this alone to average the totals in the column

A column in style 1 will let you
enter left aligned text in the column, a
column in style 2 will line up figures by
the decimal point and a column in style 3
will show the calculated total in that
cell. Definitions remain the default
until you leave that file or redefine the
maths columns.

The Math On option (Alt F7 1) is a
toggle and puts the [Math On] code in
your document. The word **Math** will flash
in the lower left hand corner of the
screen. You need this on your screen
before you can create, edit or calculate
a maths document.

Entering Text and Numbers for Maths
Use the tab key to move the cursor to
each column that you need to use. Text
will be aligned according to the
definitions you made earlier. When the
cursor enters a calculation column an
exclamation mark is displayed. In order

to make the calculation you need to press
Alt F7 2 and the result(s) will be
displayed.

Vertical Totals
When you want to add up a column
vertically to produce a total place the
cursor in the appropriate column and type
a +. Press the calculation keys (Alt F7
2) to get the total.

Automatic Recalculation
When math is on any alterations you make
to the data in the numeric columns will
automatically recalculate as soon as you
press the calculation command (Alt F7 2).

Stopping Maths Mode
As soon as you have finished calculating
turn math off (Alt F7 1).

Columns
WordPerfect provides two different sorts
of column. A newspaper column "snakes"
down one column and then up to the next

one and down again, like this:

A newspaper column   the cursor goes up
snakes up and down   to the next column
the page like this   automatically.
and when it reaches   Press Ctrl Enter to
the end of the page   move to the next
                            column yourself if
                            you like.

A parallel column is designed to keep
groups of text together in one column,
rather useful for inventories or lists of
names and addresses, like this:

Mr Morrison   The Grange   091-3465
                Little Weedham
                Nr Billenbenn
                Flowerpots

Mrs Green   12 Hillcroft Rd   092-4567
                Cranleigh
                KRO 1TT

In both cases you can move from one
column to the next using the Ctrl Enter
command. When you reach the last column,
and you can have a maximum of five, the
cursor returns to column one.

Define Columns
Before you can set up newspaper or
parallel columns they must first be
defined (Alt F7 4). The column define
menu is illustrated in Figure 7.7. First
decide whether to have the columns evenly
spaced across the whole page or not, then

Figure 7.7   Text Column Definition

   Do you wish to have evenly spaced columns? (Y/N)? N
   If yes number of spaces between columns?
   Type of columns:
      1 - Newspaper
      2 - Parallel with Block Protect

Number of text columns (2-24) 0

Column	Left	Right	Column	Left	Right
0:			13:		
1:			14:		
2:			15:		
3:			16:		
4:			17:		
5:			18:		
6:			19:		
7:			20:		
8:			21:		
9:			22:		
10:			23:		
11:			24:		
12:			25:		

the gutter size (spaces between columns) and finally the type of column you require and how many. Once these parameters have been decided a list of column positions for the left and right hand edge of the columns you specify is displayed. These figures may be overtyped but columns may not overlap.

Once columns have been defined you can invoke column mode.

Column Mode

Invoke column mode (Alt F7 3) as soon as the columns have been defined. The Col 1 message joins the status line at the base of the screen. Press Ctrl Enter to move one column to the right. As soon as the last column is reached the Ctrl Enter command will return the cursor to the first column.

To cancel column mode press Alt F7 3 once more.

```
┌─────────┐
│   F8    │          UNDERLINE
└─────────┘
```

Use this command to underline text as it
is entered onto the screen. The underline
command is a toggle and reveals the code
[U] at the start of underlining and [u]
at the end. In order to delete underline
you need to delete the [U] code. If codes
are not revealed and you try to delete an
embedded code by using the backspace or
Del key the following prompt will appear
onscreen: Delete Underline (Y/N) ? N.
Type n or any key other than Y to leave
the underline code.
     If you want to underline text
retrospectively you need to mark it as a
block first, see section on Alt F4, and
press the underline key.

```
┌─────────┐      ┌─────────┐
│  Ctrl   │      │   F8    │     PRINT
└─────────┘      └─────────┘
```

Use this command to alter the print
format of your document. This feature
lets you alter the pitch, font, line
spacing, underline style, specify the bin
you want to use in the sheet feed, insert
a printer command, number lines
automatically or turn justification on
and off. Figure 8.1 illustrates the menu
that you could receive as soon as you
press Ctrl F8:

Figure 8.1

Print Format

1 - Pitch   10
    Font   1

2 - Lines Per Inch 6

Right Justification   On
    3 - Turn Off
    4 - Turn On

Underline Style   5
    5 - Non-continuous Single
    6 - Non-continuous Double
    7 - Continuous Single
    8 - Continuous Double

9 - Sheet Feeder Bin Number 1
A - Insert Printer Command
B - Line Numbering Off

Selection: 0

All these parameters will come into
operation from the moment they are set
for that document. To alter any
parameters you need to reset them where
necessary. To delete their effect reveal
the codes (Alt F3) and delete the
corresponding code tag.

Pitch
Pitch is usually preset to 10, allowing
10 characters per inch, press 1 and
overtype this with the number of the
pitch required to alter it. Follow the
pitch number with an asterisk to denote a
proportional font. Your printer manual
will tell you which pitches it can use.

Font
There can be up to 8 fonts available,
numbered 1-8. Some daisy wheel printers
will stop when they receive the font
change code to let you change the print
wheel. When this happens you will need to
resume printing using the Shift F7 4 G
command. To see which fonts are available
change the font and type a line, change
it again and continue for all eight, then
print it. Figure 8.2 displays a typical
example of the fonts available in 10
pitch.

Lines per inch
You have the choice between 6 and 8 lines
per inch (lpi).

Figure 8.2

This is font 1
This is font 2
This is font 3
This is font 4
This is font 5
This is font 6
This is font 7
This is font 8

Justification
Remember that the default is for justification to be ON at the start of a new document so you will need to alter this parameter at the start of each file that you want to be ragged right instead.

Underline
Underline style can underline tabs (7 or 8); and produce double lines (6 or 8). The default is non-continuous single lines.

Sheet Feed
The sheet feeder option defaults to take paper from the first(or only) bin but his can be altered according to your own equipment.

Your printer manual will be able to tell you which commands it will understand for option A.

Line Numbering
The line numbering facility is preset to OFF but you could have the lines numbered for you down the page if you choose.

| Shift | | F8 | | LINE |

Use this command to alter or look at the current ruler line format for your document. Figure 8.3 displays the line format menu.

It is at this menu that you can change margins, tab settings, spacing, hyphenation parameters and align

Figure 8.3

1 2 Tabs; 3 Margins; 4 Spacing; 5 Hyphenation; 6 Align Character: 0

Figure 8.4

[HZone Set] 7,0 Off Aided; 1 On; 2 Off; 3 Set H-Zone; 4 Aided; 5 Auto: 0

characters. When you make the change a code is embedded in the text. Delete the code and its effect is deleted too.

Only text that appears after the change is affected when you alter one of the options from the menu.

Displaying the Ruler

If you want to check the current tab and margin settings for your document you could either reveal the codes (Alt F3) and look at the ruler, or open a window (Ctrl F3 1) and press up cursor followed by Enter to leave the ruler at the base of the screen. To remove this ruler press Ctrl F3 1 again but this time press the down cursor and Enter. A margin is illustrated by a curly bracket if it is in the same column as a tab or a square bracket if it stands alone. A tab stop is illustrated by a triangle. WordPerfect defaults to give a left margin in column 10 so remember to take this into account when setting tabs.

Tabs

Tabs are preset every 5 spaces but they can be altered as often as you like. The change applies to subsequent text only. To set or clear tabs press Shift F8 1. Use the cursor to move along the ruler and select positions for Left aligned, Right aligned, Decimal or Centre tabs. To set multiple tabs enter the column number for the first tab stop, followed by a comma and the interval number. Delete a tab by positioning the cursor over that tabstop on the ruler and pressing Del. If you want to delete all the tabs from the cursor position on the ruler to the right

press **Ctrl End**. Alternatively tabs may be
set by typing the number for the relevant
column and pressing **Enter**. As soon as you
have completed your tab settings press
EXIT.

Extended Tabs

This feature is only needed if the right
margin is to extend beyond column 160.
Extended tabs have been preset for every
10 spaces beginning with position 160.
Press **Shift F8 2** to display the extended
tabs message and enter the position
number of the first tab (a number between
150 and 220) followed by the interval
number. This sets the number of spaces
between each tab.

Margins

Margins are preset to columns 10 and 74.
To alter one or either of these press
Shift F8 3, type the number of the column
you want for the left margin, press **Enter**
and type the number for the right margin
and press **Enter** once more.

Spacing

WordPerfect defaults to give single
spacing. To change this press **Shift F8 4**
and enter 1.5 for one and a half spacing,
2 for double spacing and so on. The
correct spacing will be shown onscreen to
the nearest whole number.

Hyphenation

Although WordPerfect does not default to
hyphenate words automatically this
feature is available and adaptable to
your requirements. If you invoke the

hyphenation menu there are five choices
available, see Figure 8.4.

Hyphenation can be set like
justification, to operate for certain
sections of text only. At such times a
blinking - or / appears on screen and the
code [Hyph On] is used at the start and
end of the specified text. So, take the
cursor to the place where you want
hyphenation to start and press Shift F8 5
1 and Enter. As you type subsequent text
the system will "beep" each time that a
word is encountered that it considers to
be eligible for hyphenation. Take the
cursor to a suitable point for the
hyphen, incidentally it is a soft hyphen
and will therefore disappear if wordwrap
at a later stage moves both parts of the
word onto the same line, and press Esc.
If you do not want a word to be
hyphenated press Cancel and it will move
to the next line preceded by a blinking /
to remind you that it could be
hyphenated. If you want to hyphenate such
a word after all delete the blinking /.
If you want to insert a space instead of
a hyphen press Home Spacebar.

Aided hyphenation will ask for
intervention from you before hyphenation
occurs, auto hyphenation will not.

As soon as you want to end the
hyphenation zone press Shift F8 5 2.

Soft Hyphens
If you are not in hyphenation mode but
want to insert a soft hyphen into a long
word anyway use the Ctrl together with
the _ key.

Dashes
To create a double hyphen press **Home** $-$ $-$.

Minus sign
To create a minus sign press **Home** $-$.

H Zone
The Hyphenation Zone is a term referring to the number of characters that have to exceed the end of the line before the system decides whether to let wordwrap or hyphenation take place. The HZone also determines how far you can move the hyphen in the word when WordPerfect asks for hyphenation help. With justification off a small H-Zone will produce a more even right margin. The default is set to 7 for the left HZone and 0 for the right one. The smaller the zone the more hyphenation may occur.

Align Character
Use this command or **Ctrl F6** to align text to the right at a tab stop. It will also line up decimal points and may be used as a dectab.

Alt	F8	PAGE

Use this command to set parameters that govern the size and design of the printed page. Figure 8.5 illustrates the page format menu.

Figure 8.5

1   Page Number Position
2   New Page Number
3   Centre Page Top to Bottom
4   Page Length
5   Top Margin
6   Headers or Footers
7   Page Number Column Positions
8   Suppress for Current Page Only
9   Conditional End of Page
10 Widow/Orphan Protection

Page Number Position
Use this command to determine where you
want page numbers to be printed, if any.
There are 8 options available and they
apply whether you choose automatic page
numbering, starting at 1, or otherwise.
The default is 0 and gives no page
numbers for that document.

New Page Number
Use this option to number the current
page, according to the parameters set in
option 1. Enter the relevant number when
requested. Automatic numbering will then
start from this number, you are given the
choice of Roman or Arabic styles. New
page numbers are shown on the screen and
when printed out. This is especially
useful when you want to combine more than
one file at print time but work on them
separately.

Centre Page Top to Bottom
Use this command to centre the current
page from top to bottom on the paper when
it is printed.

Page Length
Use this command to set the size of the
paper and number of lines you want on it
if this differs from the default. The
default allows 54 lines on an A4 page,
which, incidentally, is 66 lines long.
When these parameters apply WordPerfect
gives you a system page break after each
54 lines that you type. A system page
break moves automatically as you cut,
copy or move text and is illustrated by a
single row of hyphens. If you want to
enter a fixed page break (hard page) the
command is **Ctrl Enter**, it is illustrated
by a double row of hyphens and can be
deleted by the **Del** key.

Top Margin
Use this command to set the top margin,
this is the amount of lines that the
printer will scroll up before starting to
print. Margins are set in half-lines and
the default is 1 inch (12 lines). Enter
the number of lines you require in the
top margin at the prompt.

Headers or Footers
Use this command to print the same text
at the top, or bottom, of every page. You
are allowed a maximum of two headers and
two footers for each document so that
they could differ on odd from even pages
if required. When you select option **6** the

following screen is shown:

Type	Occurrence
1 Header A	0 Discontinue
2 Header B	1 Every Page
3 Footer A	2 Odd Pages
4 Footer B	3 Even Pages
	4 Edit

Selection: 0   Selection: 0

Type the number for the "Type" you require, you are then asked to select an option from the "occurrences". A blank screen is displayed in which you are to enter the text for the header or footer. Press EXIT when you are finished.

Many of the usual formatting commands will apply for a header/footer, tabs, alignment, centre, bold and underline.

If you want to alter a header/footer the cursor needs to be after the relevant code before you press Alt F8 6 # 4.

To put a page number in a header/footer you need to press Ctrl B in the header/footer.

Headers will print on the first text line of each page. WordPerfect then adjusts the line length accordingly. The first line of a footer will start on the last text line of the page. If a footer is more than one line long the remainder will print in the bottom margin.

Page Number Column Positions
Use this option to define the column position for the page number position (option 1). The default is set to place

a left page number in column a 10, a
centre in column 42 and a right number in
column 74.

Suppress for Current Page Only
Use this command to turn off any
combination of page formats, set in the
current document from this menu for the
current page.

Conditional End of Page
Use this command to keep a block of text
together on the same page at all times.
You will receive a prompt that asks you
for the number of lines to keep together.

Widow/Orphan Protection
Use this command to safeguard against the
last line of a paragraph to be carried
over to the top of the next page (orphan)
and against the first line of a paragraph
to be left at the bottom of a page
(widows).

Press F9 and the merge symbol ^R is
displayed onscreen at the cursor
position. It is used to divide the
records in the secondary (data) file into
fields.

The Secondary File
The data file is created on the
workscreen like an ordinary document.
Save the file with the extension .SF
(secondary file), LIST1.SF could be a
suitable filename for you. Use it after
each field. A field can contain more than
one line. ^R on its own can be used if a
field is empty, as shown in Figure 9.1.
You can use the **sort** feature to put these
records in alphabetical order, see the
section on **Ctrl F9**.

Figure 9.1

Mr Alan Jackson^R
The Cottage^R
The Street^R
Townsville
COUNTS^R
TOW 23H^R
02-887766^R
Alan^R
^E
Mrs Betty Heron^R
Tall Trees^R
4, Waverley Gardens^R
Ellingham^R
^R
0678-7777^R
Betty^R
^E

     The data for each record must end
with the ^E symbol, press **Shift F9** for
this.

The Primary File
This is the file that contains the fixed
text to be merged with the variables
(records) from the **secondary file** (data
file). Save this file giving it a .PF
extension. Each field in the data file is
specified by means of ^F and the number
of the field within a record. The section
on **Alt F9** explains about available merge
codes. The secondary file, illustrated
above, has 8 fields within the record. Of
course you may not need to merge them all
into a matrix letter, Figure 9.2 is a
typical example.

Figure. 9.2

^F1^
^F2^
^F3^
^F4^
^F5^

Dear Madam

Further to your recent enquiry I am
pleased to send you details about our
suspended ceilings.

I look forward to hearing from you in the
near future.

Yours sincerely

Kenny Garrett

```
┌─────────┐     ┌─────────┐
│  Ctrl│     │  F9  │          MERGE/SORT
└─────────┘     └─────────┘
```

Use this command to print merge a primary
file with a secondary file and to sort
blocks of text into alphabetical
ascending or descending order. The
merge/sort menu is:

1 Merge; 2 Sort; 3 Sorting Sequences: 0

Press 1 to start a print merge. Press 2
to sort a file or a marked block of text,
the current file is the default (screen).
Option 3 lets you set the sorting
sequence. US/European sorts American and
European characters. The Scandinavian
option will also sort Scandinavian
characters too.

Sort
Use the sort feature to sort and select
lines, paragraphs or secondary merge
records from within WordPerfect. The
document that you want to sort can be on
your screen or another file on disk, when
it is sorted it can either replace the
document on screen or be sent to a file
on disk. Always save your document before
sorting.

Line Sort

Lines must be single spaced, as illustrated below:

Bury St Edmonds
Cambridge
Barnsley
Ancaster
Colchester

If you want to sort the contents of the file on your screen press Ctrl F9 2 followed by Enter to accept the current file (screen) as the sort lines. Press Enter again to accept the current file (screen) as the output file. The sort by line menu should now be displayed, if it is not press 7 (type) and 2 for line. Press 1 to begin the sort. See Fig. 9.3 for an illustration of the sort by line menu.

Perform Action

This option will begin the sort according to the parameters specified at this point.

View

This option will scroll through the document.

Keys

This option lets you define the keys as alphanumeric or numeric and indicate their exact location by field (making up a record in a data file), line and word allowing you to prioritise the words to sort on, key1 has first priority key2 has second and so on. WordPerfect needs to know the exact location of each key word.

Figure 9.3

```
-------------Sort by Line-------------

Key Typ Field Word  Key Typ Field Word Key Typ Field Word
1    a    1    1         2               3
4                        5               6
7                        8               9
Select

Action                  Order           Type of Sort
Sort                    Ascending       Line Sort

1 Perform Action; 2 View; 3 Keys; Select; 5 Action; 6 Order; 7 Type:0
```

So a file must be divided into units that
Wordperfect recognises: records, fields,
lines and words.

Record
This is the unit to be sorted. Lines that
end with a soft or hard return are taken
as records in a line sort. Paragraphs,
ending with one or more hard returns are
treated as records in a paragraph sort.
Secondary merge records are divided by
merge E (Shift F9).

Field
A **field** is used to make up a record and
applies to a particular category such as
"Company" in a data file record and will
always appear in the same position in a
record. You can have as many fields as
you like in a record as long as they are
separated with ^R, see section on **F9**. A
line ends with a soft or hard returns in
paragraphs and secondary merge files.

Word
A **word** is taken to be a string of
characters between two spaces.

Select
This option creates a select statement
with logic symbols.

Action
This lets you decide between Select and
Sort or Select Only (if a select
statement exists).

Order
This allows you to choose between

ascending and descending order for the
sort.

Sort Type
This lets you choose between Line,
Paragraph (Block) or Merge sorts.

Block Sort
This also known as paragraph sort. If you
want to sort a specific part of the text
it must be marked as a block first, see
Alt 4. Again the keys to press to sort
this text are Ctrl F9, after which the
sort menu appears onscreen directly.
Press 1 to perform the sort.

Secondary Merge Sort
Use this feature to sort the records in a
data file that you would use as part of a
mailmerge.

| Shift | | F9 | MERGE E |

Use this command to separate the records
in a **Secondary File** to be merged with its
corresponding **Primary File** during merge.
The ^E symbol appears on the screen on a
separate line and the cursor hops
straight down to the following line ready
for the start of the next record.
Figure 9.1 illustrates this.

| Alt | | F9 | MERGE CODES |

Wordperfect gives you 14 different merge
commands that will help you to automate

your merge as much as possible. The ^F
code is probably the most frequently used
and specifies the position of the
corresponding field data from the record
in the resulting merged document, see
Figure 9.2. As soon as you press the Alt
F9 command the menu shown in Figure 9.4
is displayed.

^C will temporarily stop the merge so
that text can be entered from the
keyboard. Press the **Merge R** keys to
continue with the merge.

^D will insert the current date (if
the current date was set accurately
during booting up) at this point in the
merged document.

^E marks the end of each record in
the secondary file (Shift F9 has the same
effect), see Figure 9.1.

^Fn^ merges the document from the
specified field into the document being
created.

^G is used in the sequence *^Gmacro
name^G* and starts the named macro at the
end of the merge.

^N tells WordPerfect to get the next
record from the secondary file.

^O is used in the sequence
^Omessage^O to display the message on the
status line during printing. This command
is usually used in conjunction with ^C.

^P tells WordPerfect to start again
from the beginning using the primary file
named between a pair of ^Ps. If no
filename is entered at this point the
current filename becomes the default.

^Q stops the merge at this point. It
may be used in either a primary or a
secondary file.

^R is used to mark the end of a file
in a secondary file.
^S is used in the sequence
^S*filename*^S to change to a named
secondary file at this point.
^T tells WordPerfect to send all
text merged to that point to the printer.
^U will update (rewrite) the screen.
^V lets you transfer merge codes
into the document being created.
Use the ^N^P^P combination at the
end of the primary file to tell
Wordperfect not to insert an extra page
break since the printer will
automatically advance straight to the
next page when it finishes the letter. If
you fail to use this command the system
may throw a blank page between each
letter.

```
┌─────────┐
│ F10     │     SAVE
└─────────┘
```

Use this command to name and save the
current document and return to it
immediately at the same cursor position.

Document Summary
Sometimes the document summary screen
will be displayed. You are able to enter
the name of the author, operator and any
comments. Press **F7** (Exit) to leave the
summary. You do not have to enter
anything in the summary if you do not
want to, in which case you need to press
F7 until the document returns onscreen
and the **Document to be Saved:** prompt
appears at the base of the screen. If the
document has not been named previously
you will be required to name it at this
point and press **Enter** to return to the
document.

Save Block of Text Out to a New File
To save a portion of text out to a new
file you need to mark it as a block first
of all. See the section on **Alt F4** if
necessary. As soon as the entire block
has been marked (highlighted) press **F10**
and the **Block Name:** prompt is displayed.
Enter the name you require for the block
of text and press **Enter**. To stop the
Block On message from flashing at the
base of the screen press **F1** (cancel).

A macro is a piece of text or command
that you store and reuse simply and
quickly. It is a time-saving device and
can be used to perform your sorting or
mailmerge commands in addition to the
more simple repetitive keystrokes, such
as retrospective underlining for example.
        First you need to define the macro.
Press **Ctrl F10** and you will be asked
Macro to Define:. In order to use the
default macro file press **Alt P**. Now you
can enter the keystrokes that you want to
include in your macro. For example to do
retrospective underline to a whole line
you would press **Home <- <- F8 Home ->
-> F8**. The words **Macro Def** flash in the
bottom left hand corner of the screen to
remind you that every keystroke you make
is being recorded in the macro. As soon
as you have defined the contents of the
macro press **Ctrl F10**. To invoke a macro
press **Alt F10** and name the macro you
require. The default is the **ALTP.MAC**
macro used by pressing **Alt P** when you
defined the macro initially. All macro
files are given the .MAC extension. You
may store as many macros as you like on
disk if you name them differently from
ALTP.MAC.
        Use macros to store *any* keystrokes
you wish to record and reuse. It is very
useful to store formatting commands as a
macro, especially if a certain style
requires odd margins, pitch, page length
and fonts, like a publishers manuscript.

Simply call the macro onscreen every time that you start a new document.

```
┌─────────┐     ┌─────────┐
│ Shift   │     │  F10    │     RETRIEVE
└─────────┘     └─────────┘
```

Use this command to call a previously
created document onto the workscreen.
This could be used when you want to
combine files and when you want to recall
a previously created document into the
blank workscreen. As soon as you press
Shift F10 the **Document to be Retrieved:**
prompt is displayed so enter the name of
the document, preceded by drive letter if
appropriate and press **Enter**.

Retrieve File from List Files Menu
A file may also be retrieved from the
List Files Menu. The entire file will
then come onto the workscreen at the
cursor position before F5 was pressed.

```
┌─────────┐     ┌─────────┐
│  Alt    │     │  F10    │     MACRO
└─────────┘     └─────────┘
```

Use this command, as explained in the
section on **Ctrl F10** (macro def), to
invoke a previously saved macro. The
Macro: prompt will appear onscreen after
which you must enter the name of the
macro required. Remember they all end
with the .MAC extension.

LIST OF FUNCTIONS

SHIFT FUNCTIONS - Press SHIFT and a
Function key.

F1	1	Superscript
F1	4	Advance Up
F1	5	Advance Down
F1	3	Overstrike
F1	2	Subscript
F2		Search Backwards
F3		Switch Document
F3		Case Conversion (Block on)
F4		Indent - left and right
		(followed by bkspce)
F5	1	Insert date as text
F5	3	Insert function
F5		Date Menu
F5	2	Date format
F6		Centre
F7	4 2	Display Printers and Fonts
F7	4 D	Display all Print Jobs
F7	4 C	Cancel Print jobs
F7	3 3	Binding Width
F7	4 5	Stop Print
F7	6 2	Preview Page
F7	6 1	Preview Document
F7	6	Preview
F7	4 2	Select Printers and Fonts
F7	4 1	Select Print Options
F7	3 2	Number of copies
F7	4 R	Rush print job
F7	3 1	Printer Number
F7		Print (Block On)
F7	4 G	Go - Resume/Start printing
F7	4 P	Print document
F7	3	Print Options
F7	4	Printer Control
F7	1	Full Text Print
F7		Print Menu

```
F7 2          Page Print
F7 5          Type-through
F8 6          Alignment Character
F8 3          Margins
F8 1 or 2     Tab set (L, C, R, D)
F8            Line format Menu
F8 4          Spacing
F8 5 5        Auto Hyphenation
F8 5 4        Aided Hyphenation
F8 5 3        H-Zone set
F8 5 2        Hyphenation On
F8 5 1        Hyphenation Off
F8 1 or 2     Extended Tabs (160-250)
F9            Merge E
F9            Merge E
F10           Retrieve Document
Tab           Margin Release
```

Alt - Press Alt key plus a Function key

```
F1            Thesaurus
F2            Replace
F3            Reveal Codes toggle
F4            Block On
F5            Strikeout (Block On)
F5 5          Index
F5            List (Block on)
F5 0 5        Define Index
F5 0 7        Edit Table of Authorities Full
              Form
F5 0 1        Define Paragraph/Outline
              Numbering
F5 1          Outline
F5 4          Short Form
F5 0 4        Define Table of Authorities
F5 0 3        Define List
F5 0 2        Define Table of Contents
F5 2          Paragraph Number
F5 0          Mark Text Options
F5 3          Redline
```

F5		Table of Contents (Block On)
F5	0 6	Remove all Redline Markings and Strikeout in text
F5		Mark Text
F5	0 8	Generate Tables and Index
F6		Flush right
F7	2	Math Define
F7	1	Math On
F7	3	Column on/off toggle
F7	5	Column Display
F7		Maths Menu
F7	4	Column Define
F8	7	Page Number Position
F8	4	Page Length
F8	6	Headers or Footers
F8	2	New Page Number
F8	3	Centre Page Top to Bottom
F8	A	Widow/Orphan
F8	5	Top Margin
F8	9	Conditional End of Page
F8	8	Suppress Page Format (Current Page Only)
F8		Block Protect (Block On)
F9		Merge codes C, D, F, G, N, O, P, Q, S, T, U, V
F10	.	Macro
CONTROL	-	Press CONTROL plus a function key
-		Soft hyphen
<---		Delete word
End		Delete to end of line
Enter		Hard Page
F1		Go to DOS/shell
F1		Shell
F2		Spell
F2		Word Count
F3	4	Colours
F3	2	Line Draw

F3	3	Ctrl/Alt key mapping
F3	1	Lines in window
F3		Screen Menu
F3	1	Split Screen/window
F3	5	Auto Rewrite
F3	Enter	Rewrite
F4	1	Move sentence
F4		Move Menu
F4		Block
F4	5	Retrieve text (Move)
F4		Column Cut/copy (block on)
F4		Rectangle Cut/copy (block on)
F4	4	Retrieve column (Move)
F4	2	Move paragraph
F4	3	Move page
F4		Append Block (block on)
F4	6	Retrieve rectangle (Move)
F5		Text In/Out Menu
F5	3	Retrieve DOS text file with soft returns
F5	5	Retrieve locked document
F5	2	Retrieve DOS text file with hard returns
F5	4	Save locked document
F5	1	Save DOS text file
F5		DOS text file Menu
F5	D	Display summary and comments
F5	B	Create comment
F5	A	Create/edit Summary
F5	7	Save in WordPerfect 4.1 format
F5	6	Save in generic WP format
F5	C	Edit comment
F5	4	Save Text out to a new file
F5	5	Retrieve text from a different file
F6		Tab Align to the left
F7	5	Create Endnote
F7	6	Edit endnote
F7	4	Options (20 available)
F7	2	Edit Footnote

99

F7	1	Create Footnote
F7		Footnote Menu
F7	3	New Number (Footnote)
F8	9	Sheet Feeder Bin Number
F8	2	Lines per inch
F8	1	Font
F8		Print Format
F8	3	Justification off
F8	4	Justification on
F8	A	Insert Printer Command
F8		Block Protect (block on)
F8	1	Pitch
F8	B	Line Numbering Off
F8		Underline Style
F8	1	Font
F9	3	Sorting sequences
F9	2	Sort
F9		Merge
PgDn		Delete to end of page
F10		Macro Definition

FUNCTION KEYS ALONE

-		Hyphen
<---		Backspace
Del		Delete
Enter		Enter/hard return
Esc		Escape/cancel
F1		Undelete
F1		Cancel
F1		Cancel hyphenation
F2		Search
F3		Help
F4		Indent left
F5	Enter	Text in (List files)
F5	=	Create Directory
F5	Enter	Copy list files
F5	Enter	Retrieve (List files)
F5	Enter	Rename (List files)
F5	Enter	Print (List files)

```
F5 Enter    Change Directory
F5 Enter    Delete Directory (List files)
F5 Enter    Look
F5 Enter    List files
F5 Enter    Delete (List files)
F5 Enter    Word Search
F6          Bold toggle
F7          Exit
F8          Underline
F9          Merge R
F10         Save
Home spc    Hard Space
Home -      Minus sign
Home        Home
Tab         Tab
```

INDEX

DIARY   AB – CAL.FIL